Rumi's MATHNAVI

Rumi's
Mathnavi

A Theatre Adaptation

Joe Martin

مولانا

Coyote Arts / Albuquerque

Rumi's Mathnavi © 1998, 2003, 2007, and 2020 by Joe Martin and Open Theatre/DC. Front cover photograph © 2007 Joe Martin. Author photograph © 2007 Lisa Lias. Production photographs © 2005 Page Carr.

Transliterated Persian passages by Lida Saeedian.

Joe Martin also writes as Yousef Daoud.

Book design by Jordan Jones. Cover design by Linda Zupcic.

Second edition.

10 9 8 7 6 5 4 3 2 1

ISBN 978-1-58775-033-5 (paper)
ISBN 978-1-58775-021-2 (electronic)
Library of Congress Control Number: 2020942557
SAN 254-0126

> Coyote Arts LLC
> PO Box 6690
> Albuquerque, NM 87197-6690
> www.coyote-arts.com

This play is fully protected by international copyright law, and may not be performed without the expressed permission of the author or his agent.

For all professional and amateur performance rights, contact:

> Tonda Marton
> The Marton Agency
> One Union Square West, Room 818
> New York, NY 10003-3303
> tonda@martonagcy.org or martonagcy@aol.com

*For Professor Abdul Aziz Said
and the Center for Global Peace*

Production History

Rumi's MATHNAVI was first performed as readers' theatre-with-music by Open Theatre/DC at the Center for International Theatre Exchange (CITE), in the Experimental Theatre, American University, co-sponsored by the Center for Global Peace and the Department of Performing Arts, December 7, 1998.

>Directed by JOE MARTIN
>Choreography by CHRISTEL STEVENS
>Music Direction by NADR MAJD
>Lighting by KRISTEN RUTHERFORD

The cast included:

>DAVID HARSHEID   CAROLINE MCGEE
>STEVEN WILHITE   CARLOS GONZALES
>ROBERT BOSCO   CHRISTEL STEVENS
>LISA LIAS

The second readers' theatre production of *Rumi's* MATHNAVI also took place at CITE, on December 6, 1999.

>Directed by JOE MARTIN
>Choreographed by CHRISTEL STEVENS
>Music by SHUBHA SANKARAN (Surbahar) and DEBU NAYAK (Tablas)

The cast included:

>DAVID HARSHEID   SARAH PLEYDELL
>NAGAMALLA JAYAKER   STEVEN WILHITE
>CARLOS GONZALES   CHRISTEL STEVENS
>SARAH TRUOG

An experimental multi-lingual version of segments of the script and some additional parables was produced at La MaMa Experimental Theatre Club at the Annex theatre, running from September to October 2000 as *Selections from "Rumi's* MATHNAVI." The selections were directed and designed by Mahmood Karimi

Hakak; with music by Mehti Meigani; with the following company performing as ensemble, and contributing renderings of texts in foreign languages.

Nikki Bell	Tania Ritter
Zeynep Bilik	Shigeko Suga
Rob Laqui	Kayo Takahashi
Carlos Linares	Brandon Welch
Manya Meigani	Christel Stevens
Luis Tareke Ortiz	

Rumi's Mathnavi in the present version was produced by Open Theatre/DC in a touring production which opened at the Hartke Theatre, Washington DC on February 19, and ran through March 21, 2005, with the following cast:

Kim Curtis	Husamuddin, Moses, the Helmsman, ensemble
Bette Cassatt	The Seeker, the Shepherd, ensemble
Nick Scott	The Bedouin, the Sufi's Visitor, the Snake Catcher, the Cow-Owner, ensemble
Jai Khalsa	The Wife at the Fruit Tree, Indian Dancer, the Moon-gazer, ensemble
Elizabeth Jernigan	The Bedouin's Wife, the Sufis' Servant, ensemble
Lee Ordeman	Sultan's Official, the Linguist, Omar, the Serpent, King David, ensemble
Jamahl Rahman	Court Official, the Husband at the Fruit Tree, ensemble
Brandon Welch	The Sultan, Bazaar Barker, the Do-Nothing, ensemble

Directed by Joe Martin
Choreography by Christel Stevens
Music by The Hamnava Group and Kasem Davoudian
Scenography by Joe Martin
Costumes by Christel Stevens
Lighting by Tom Donahue
Photography by Page Carr

Contents

Production History	vi
Notes on Rumi and His Meaning for Spiritual Evolution	3
Characters	8
Production Note	9

Act I   *11*

Prologue	12
Song of the Ney	16
The Bedouin and His Wife: Part I	18
The Pear Tree of Illusion	22
The Bedouin and His Wife: Part 2 — "Men and Women"	26
The Story of an Exchange Between the Linguist and the Helmsman	32
The Bedouin and His Wife: Part 3 — The Water Carrier	35
The Elephant in the Dark House	40
How Moses Took Offense at a Shepherd's Prayer	44

Act II   *51*

How Some Sufis Sold a Traveler's Donkey to Pay for a Night of Music	51
The Person Who Imagined Seeing the New Moon	59
The Frozen Snake	61
The Man Who Prayed for an Income without Labor in the Time of King David	66
Rites of Return: Wedding the Beloved	83

Afterword: Why Put Rumi on Stage?   *87*

Photos: Page Carr

Notes on Rumi and His Meaning for Spiritual Evolution

The poet and spiritual master Jelaluddin Rumi (1207–1273 CE) some years ago became the best selling poet in the United States, and continues to be. In much of the Islamic world he is known as Mowlâna: "Our Master." A thirteenth century poet born in the area of the old Persian Empire, today Balkh Afghanistan, and who lived most of his life in Turkey writing some of the greatest Persian poetry and spiritual discourses, finds a sudden and massive resurgence of interest: this strange development has been a topic of much discussion lately among poets and scholars. Some attribute it to New Age thinking, or millenarianism. Others, reading the free, accessible and amusing Coleman Barks English versions of Rumi may sense he is working in something like the traditions of Whitman, Blake and even Allen Ginsberg, and thus has appeal for the new "spiritual seekers."

The poet and author Andrew Harvey suggests that Rumi's spiritual method through deep devotion to his teacher and spiritual beloved, Shams-i Tabriz, was an ingenious approach to the mystical path. It set off an explosion in this former Muslim and Sufi scholar who had never really written poetry, so that his *Divan-i Shams* (or

Divan-i Kabir) comprises seven volumes and 20,000 lines of mystic ghazals (our closest equivalent is the sonnet form) and his *Mathnavi* is six books of fifteen thousand verse lines. But Harvey also thinks that when we read or hear Rumi, we can find the deeper answers for the plight of the planet, our reasons to care for the natural world, and the evolution of our own consciousness. The most impressive scholar of Sufism in the West, Anne Marie Schimmel, in *The Triumphal Sun* has placed him as a sort of vortex through which older traditions of Islamic and pre-Islamic mysticism pass, before fanning out on the other side into the coherent system of spiritual practice and psychology we call Sufism today. She finds, however, that much of the startling imagery that has made him one of the world's four or five most important poets derives from the *Qur'an*. She also finds that his use of unexpected paradox resembles that of the Zen Buddhist writers and teachers.

The *Mathnavi* derives its name from the twenty two syllable lines that Rumi recited by and large spontaneously to his scribe Husamuddin Chelebi, while walking in the gardens of Konya, or spinning around a pole, or seated in contemplation. It weaves together ancient and original parables, stemming from the many literary and religious traditions, then reflects on platonic philosophy, the science of Galen, and then rises to lyric eloquence in descriptions of the "unseen" world based upon some very vivid and earthy metaphors. The *Mathnavi* is sung in chai houses and homes from the Middle East to Central Asia to the Indian Subcontinent. Some of its parables are told as ribald jokes.

The parables are also summoned up to teach lessons by teachers of Sufism, and gnostic Islam. Yet while it is popular, it is perplexing. The structure goes from story-telling, to commentary on those stories, to yet another story as an example for the commentary, to a lyric sidetrack of a poet burning in the cooking pot of love. Then the poet might warn the listener that he has "come to the edge of the roof" and will cut off his discourse, only to return to the parable he was telling twenty pages earlier.

Rumi almost never mentions by name the philosophy of "unity of being" (*wahdhāt-al wūjūd*) which lies at the heart of Sufism. For that matter, it is the central idea in the work of the famous Andalusian Sufi Ibn Al-Arabi, known as "the greatest Master" (1165–1240), whose followers used the term extensively, though he preferred not to use it in his writing. As Kabir Helminski, the American representative of the Mevlevi Sufi order founded by Rumi (known to many Americans as the "whirling dervishes") told me: "He didn't have to mention it. It is everywhere in Rumi." The idea that each of us carries something "the same" in us — "pure water to the ocean" as he sometimes says — that we are all fundamentally related to all other beings, and even to the life of particles and energies that "live" in so-called inanimate matter – that we are all part of one cosmic evolution: this can be found everywhere in his poetry. So the "prophetic tradition" so important to Rumi, that everywhere one looks one can see the face of the Divine, tells us something fundamental about his works.

Yet Rumi, like Shakespeare in the Western tradition of great poetry, knew that human beings can't suddenly make themselves spiritually or fully conscious beings, or even true lovers. He knew that they could talk a lot, and read a lot about these things. But the problem for him was one of experience. Perhaps that is why, during many years investigating his work, those of us working to shape this material for live performance, have discovered that he returns time and again to the market place. It is the place of selling and buying, of bickering and lawsuits, of chance meetings in the corridors of perfumes leading to earthly love and secret crimes; tales of officials, merchants, beggars and dervishes; as well as tales of the officials of the ruling classes; of Moses, Jesus and Mary, the Prophet Mohammad, and the chivalrous heart of Ali. Yet he has also the Shakespearean ability to scour society and the world of human beings from top to bottom, as he teaches the way to peace, both inner and outer, and draws us away from the trap of the grasping, domineering self — or ego — through the gate of the heart.

✦

This adaptation is ninety-five percent Rumi's own words in translation. Even the frame device of using Rumi's amanuensis for the *Mathnavi*, Husammudin Chelebi, allowed us in the stagings to use Rumi's words, for he was not only Rumi's disciple, but leader of his lineage after his death. Furthermore, as he says in the text, Rumi claimed the words were passing to him from Husamuddin, as he gave them verbal shape and Husamuddin wrote them down. This has to do with Sufi methodology in spiritual experience, about which the reader or audiences will need to search elsewhere for more information. As one reads the six books of the *Mathnavi*, the poet will make constant side comments, exhortations, words of thanks and praise to Husammuddin by name, in Rumi's provocative almost "post-modern" fashion. Thus, the majority of the text spoken by the character of Husamuddin in the script is from the *Mathnavi*, especially its commentary sections. This is to a lesser extent true of the Seeker, as well. The presence of the Seeker is justified by the implied presence of the seeker (reader) or listener. The poet begins the work by stating that the text exists "for the seeker on the path."

The device is set up to allow for the strange structure the poet uses. I wanted to give a taste of how his parables stop, give way to other parables, disappear into commentary, take fire into mystic, lyric passages, and then return to a previous story. Only with this can the audience or reader get a taste of what the complete poem is like. It is wrapped around itself. It is hologram with each fragment containing the whole — like our existence itself.

The twenty two syllable line, with middle and end rhyme, which is a verse line for singing called a "mathnavi" (meaning the poem was always meant to be performed as well as read) was ignored in Reynolds Nicholson's lovingly loyal but somewhat Edwardian (and semi-Shakespearean) translation of the entire poem. He wanted to get as many levels of meaning as possible, which rhyme renders difficult. Nicholson is the basis for this adaptation. This text contains shorter lines, each one creating for the actor a "turn of idea" and a place to breathe. Choral scenes generally have four beats (feet) or three. The "Song of the Ney," which is the opening of the poem, the only part that Rumi wrote down, is my own translation from the Persian, and I have tried to get a sense of the rhyme and half-rhyme of the work, and the line breaks, for that section.

The character of the Seeker should evolve on her path through the *Mathnavi*, adding a dimension of forward progress in the performance. That the Seeker here is a woman should cause no difficulty for people of any faith (or those who claim none). The emphasis is on the name for the divine used by Sufis, especially Rumi's indirect mentor, Faruddin Attar: *an dhat,* or "that Essence," a name for the divine that is feminine.

— Joe Martin

Characters

Husamuddin Chelebi, the Poet's scribe: the Teacher
The Seeker/Young Woman, Disciple, marrying into the Poet's family
Singer
The Bedouin
Bedouin's Wife
The Husband at The Pear Tree
The Woman at The Pear Tree, his wife
Court Official One
Court Official Two
The Caliph of Baghdad
The Linguist
Helmsman
Bazaar Barker
Indian Dancer
Moses, played by Husamuddin
Shepherd, played by the The Seeker
The Visitor
Servant
Dervish One
Dervish Two
Dervish Three
Dervish Four
The Moon-Gazer
Omar
Do-Nothing
Owner-of-the-Cow
King David
& Chorus, which is also:
> Musicians, Merchants, Viziers and Courtiers, Fish Wives, Crowd in the Market, Hindu Elephant Exhibitors, Dervishes, Mob in Jerusalem, etc.

Production Note

Persian passages appear in the text. These are optional and intended for use by the chorus or a Persian singer, in parallel with English, to convey Rumi's "voice."

RUMI is never to appear in the performance of the poem: but his presence must be felt.

Photo: Page Carr

Act I

Time/Space: Konya, Seljuk capital of Rum in Anatolia, and the whole world. Thirteenth century the present, and all times. A large circular or octagonal or hexagonal space covered with rugs or mats that cover the circular playing area. A low platform at one end of the circle between the spectators' risers, for musicians and possibly the singer. This may also become a stage in the "market place" on which the Bazaar Barker and others may stand.

The spectators enter into seating surrounding the ensemble, or Chorus, who are seated silently, motionless, in a circle. The circle defines the empty space before them. The silence remains until the last audience member goes silent from awareness of their own activity in the emptiness.

An illuminated manuscript is on a small table covered with a woven rug. It is illuminated at center in a shaft of light. This shaft of light will come and go as the book becomes the center of focus, and when the focus is thrown elsewhere. Music plays. Optionally, the ensemble may enter and sit at this point.[1]

---

[1] Choruses will usually be accompanied by percussion, or music. All Persian is sung.

Prologue

Husamuddin enters from one side and is met by the Seeker (A young woman) at the center on either side of the book.

The ensemble begins whispering the introduction to the Mathnavi, perhaps in several languages, which grows into a sea of whispers from the Chorus. After a minute, Husamuddin begins speaking the text clearly, his voice rising above the susurrations of the others.

Chorus (then Husamuddin)

"This is the Book of the Mathnavi, which is the roots of the roots of the roots of the Religion in respect of its unveiling the mysteries of attainment to Truth … The likes of the light thereof is as a niche in which is a candle shining with radiance brighter than the dawn. It is the heart's paradise, having fountains and boughs … for the travelers on the Path …"

Silence.

Seeker/Young Woman

I remember a funeral. Huge crowds jamming the gates. Muslims, Jews, Christians, Greeks, Turks.

Husamuddin

You're remembering our master's funeral, which he referred to as his wedding. It was his wedding with the other side. Your wedding, however, takes place on this side — in this place.

SEEKER

My wedding will be in this place?

HUSAMUDDIN

You are marrying into his spiritual line. Here he instructed others in the mystic rite of "turning." Over there his son recorded his table talk and teaching. Outside in the garden, and down that street, I transcribed the book: an infinite poem, with no end and no beginning. This is the beginning of what you should know.

He indicates a large illuminated manuscript on a low table in the center of the carpets.

SEEKER

You recorded all of this?

HUSAMUDDIN

You've been asked to know passages by heart.

SEEKER

Yes.

HUSAMUDDIN

This poem passed through him like light. It is now my task to start you on the path to that light.

SEEKER

Where does this light come from?

HUSAMUDDIN

Nowhere.

Young Woman

How did he find this light that comes from nowhere?

Husamuddin

First it came—from Shams. Shams of Tabriz his beloved and friend. Shams, "the Sun." He was perfect mirror in which the Master could see his own light—before the day he vanished forever. From that separation our Master created his three thousand ghazals.

Young Woman

They say you were his source. They say that book records him talking to you.

Husamuddin

In fact, he often told me the words were my words. But the words came when Shams vanished, and the Master died. That is, he first time.

Young Woman

How often can a person die?

Husamuddin

Every moment.

> *He opens the book.*
>
> *Suddenly stalls and canopies start opening on all sides. The people in this "market" are trying to sell their stories. Even so, there is bickering and bargaining, eating and tea being served. This bazaar takes over the space. The cacophony of stories in many tongues turns the space into a verbal "Tower of Babel." This continues as long as necessary for this Market Place to establish itself. The chorus may actually try to sell the rugs to the audience.*

Abruptly: the CHORUS *stops in a freeze. The* SINGER *steps forward from the musicians platform, facing* HUSAMUDDIN *and the* SEEKER *from across the space.*

SEEKER

Who is that?

HUSAMUDDIN

The singer. The poem can be sung or spoken. If you hear it one way it's a symphony. It's an ocean. If you hear it another way, it's the sound of a single reed flute.

SEEKER

Where are we?

HUSAMUDDIN

It is the market. The poem takes you to the marketplace, again and again.

SEEKER

I thought you said the poem was light, like the sun.

HUSAMUDDIN

You can't simply jump into the sun. This is the center of buying, selling, toil and livelihood. The center of human existence. Now recite, "Song of the Ney."

✦

The frieze breaks, and the CHORUS *sit on their cushions around the carpet. The* SINGER *and musicians perform the first stanzas of the* MATHNAVI *in Persian, then:*

Song of the Ney

Chorus & Seeker

Listen to the ney tell its tale
Complaining of separation:

Since the time I was cut from my bed of reeds
Man and woman have moaned through me

To tell my tale I tear open my heart
Torn open by love, by being apart

Each soul straying far from her source
Longs for the oneness before divorce

To every gathering I went moaning
The happy and sad together joining

From their own point of view they became my friend
And sought in vain my secret within

The things I say, my secret lies near
But the senses lack light to see or hear

Soul from body and body from soul
Don't hide. Not all may see the soul

The sound in the ney is not wind but fire
Those lacking that fire let their being expire

The fire of love was given the ney

The ferment of love was given the wine

The ney's a comrade for severed friends
The veil of our tears its music rends

Who's seen a poison or cure like the ney?
Who's seen a consoler or muse like the ney?

The ney tells a tale of blood on the Path
Of Majnun's love that drove him mad

The senseless are those confided the sense
For the ear only buys what tongues advise

Our days run out in regret for our gains
They pass hand in hand with grief and pain

If our days should end, say: "Fine. Never fear."
O You — You remain — purest of pure.

All but the fish get bored of the water
All without bread have a long day ahead

None who are raw understand the ripe
So cut short this talk. Farewell!

✦

The Bedouin and His Wife: Part I

The Chorus *is seated on the outside edge of the circle of carpets.*

On either side of the small center table sit the Bedouin *and his* Wife, *on the rugs.*

Husamuddin

In former days there was a Caliph
who'd raised the banner of largess and liberal thought,
who had removed poverty and want from the world.
In this world of dust he was the zephyr and rain.
He was the center where the source of all was on display.
His gate and doorway was the point
to which those in need turned.
He was the water of life and the ocean of plenty.
He was the salvation of many an
Arab and foreigner.

Emerging from the "bedouin tent," far out on the desert.

Wife

We are suffering all this poverty and hardship.
The whole world's happy.
It's only us who are unhappy.
We have no bread: all we've got is despair and envy to chew on.
We have no drink: our only water is tears.
We imagine the moon is a pie in a pan,
and lift our heads in hunger for it.

The poorest of the poor are put off by our poverty.
We live in eternal night in doubt about our next meal.
Strangers and family have started to flee us.
If I beg a handful of beans from someone, he says,
"Be quiet, you pestering bat."
What gifts can we ever give? We are always the beggars.
For dinner we try to butcher the gnats in the air.
If we get any more guests, as I'm living,
soon as he's sleeping I'll pinch his ratty coat.

Bedouin

How long will you be waiting for our harvest in the desert?
What is left of our life? Our lives are mostly over.
Sensible people don't look at debit or credit.
They'll both pass away like a river.
Whether life's pure water or muddy, don't talk about it.
It doesn't last more than a moment.
In this world thousands live in contentment,
without being jerked up and down by worry.
All this grief in our hearts rises out of the vapor
and dust of our existence — the winds of desire.
Listen: each ache in your body is a piece of death.
You can fend off that piece of death, if you've got the means.
When you can't flee from the pieces of death any more,
you can bet the whole thing'll be dumped on your head.
Sheep are driven from the plains to town:
the fatter they get, the quicker they're killed.
The night is past and it's dawn. My God!
How long will you keep up this talk about money
You should be the mate of my soul.
One shoe should match the other.

The Wife

How long will you spout these phony lines, you know-it-all?
Look at your self if you want to see something shameful!
Pride is ugly, and all the uglier in beggars.
Your house is fragile as a spider's.
People in glass houses don't throw stones.
When has that "light of contentment" been in your soul?
Contentment like that is the greatest treasure.
Don't go around bragging — you grief of my life!
Don't call me your soul mate — and cut out the show of affection.
I'm not the mate of a fraud.
Don't give me that contemptuous look!
Or I'll tell everyone about your secret flaws.
You think you understand things so much better than me.
But have you ever really taken a good look at me,
this brainless woman you see here?
Oh — you are both the snake and the charmer — amazing!
The charmer chants a spell on the snake —
but meanwhile the snake's casting a spell on him.
You're trying to put a trance of fear in me with the name of God
to make me confused and ashamed!

Bedouin

Are you a woman — or the father of sorrow?
My pride is in my poverty, don't give me your tongue-lashings.
The rich merchant is sunk in vice up to his ears.
But the merchant has money to cover his vices.
Because in a world where grasping's the norm,
the greedy man doesn't see his vice.
Lust for gain is the bond of the hearts of men.
And if a beggar speaks a word of pure gold,
his wares will not make it to the shop.

The concept of spiritual poverty is beyond you.
Don't look on poverty with contempt.
If I catch snakes — as you say — it's to extract fangs
to save them from getting their heads bashed in.
I don't chant my spell to fulfill my lusts.
I have smashed such lust in the ground.
You are sitting way up on the pear tree of illusion:
climb down and get rid of your skewed vision.
When you spin round and round and get dizzy,
you see the house spinning — but you're the thing that's spinning.

The Pear Tree of Illusion

> **Seeker** *(to Husamuddin)*

Pear tree?

> *A Man and a Woman enter beneath the great pear tree.*

> **Husamuddin**

Once a woman desired to embrace her lover
in the presence of her foolish husband.
So the woman said to her husband:

> **Woman**

You lucky man. I'm going to climb the tree and gather fruit.

> *She climbs to a fair height above the space.*

> **Husamuddin**

As soon as the wife had climbed the tree,
when from the top she looked in her husband's direction,
she burst into tears.

> **Wife**

Oh, you deceiving bastard!
Who is that girl you're lying on top of over there!
You thought I wouldn't see your secret woman!

Husband

It's not true. You must've lost your mind.
Look! There's no one down here in the field but me.

Wife

Oh ho! It's she who's on top and you on the bottom?

Husband

Listen. Now you come down from that tree.
Your mind has flipped and you're getting soft in the noggin!

The WOMAN climbs down.

Husband

I'll get the fruit. Leave it to me.

He climbs up. The WIFE brings her LOVER out of hiding, and draws him down to her.

Husband *(in the tree)*

Hey! You whore! Who is that climbing on top of you!

Wife

It's not true! There's no one here but me.
Listen: you're going mad, soft in the head — don't talk rubbish!

Husband

I see you. I see what you're doing with him!

Wife

That's what you see from the pear tree.
From the top of the pear tree

I was seeing things just like that, you cuckold!
Listen: climb down, and you'll see there is nothing here.
It's all an illusion caused by the pear tree.

✦

Husamuddin

Jokes can teach you a thing or two.
Don't get caught up with the form of the joke.
To clowns all serious matters are jokes.
To the wise all jokes are serious matters.
Lazy people seek the pear tree,
but it's a long way to a greater pear tree.

Chorus

Climb down from the pear tree
on which you've become dazzled and numbed with visions.
This tree is the place of ego and self-existence,
where the squinting eye sees things crooked.

Husamuddin

When you come down from the pear tree,
your thoughts, words and vision will clear up.
Then you'll see this pear tree's become a tree of fortune,
with boughs that reach to the seventh heaven.

Chorus

Humility lies in climbing down,
you will be given true vision.
After that, climb back up the pear tree,
transformed and turned green by the divine word: Be!

Husamuddin

You will be a Moses at the burning bush.
The fire of illumination makes it come to leaf.
Its boughs cry, "I am the Light"

Seeker

But ... What the man saw when he was in the tree was not an illusion.

Husamuddin

This is a parable. It resembles reality
Adequately for our purposes.

The Bedouin and His Wife: Part 2 — "Men and Women"

Wife

You see through all delusion do you?

Bedouin

Mohammad, they say — peace be upon him —
was a mirror polished by the divine hand.
He said: "Both Turk and Indian see in me
something which exists in themselves."
Cut out those sour looks —
if you look around you'll see thousands with contented souls,
plunged in an ocean of honey.
Look, and you'll see hundreds of thousands
of bitterly suffering souls steeped in rose-syrup —
each one herself like a rose.
If only you could understand — so when I speak from the heart
the words of my soul could reach you!
These words are milk in the soul's breast:
It won't flow without a being to suck the breast.
When the audience is thirsty and hungry,
the actor, even if he's good as dead, becomes eloquent.

Wife

Good as dead — your own words.

Bedouin

Listen, stop this quarreling! Stop side-tracking.
And if you won't, then stop living with me.
Do I have time or space for bickering about
"this is good — this is bad"?
If you'll shut up, fine. If not, I'm ready to take action —
and this very minute I'm going to leave my house and home for good!

Silence. The wife begins weeping.

Wife

I never thought I'd hear those words from your mouth.
I expected more of you than that.

He begins to gather his things The wife becomes distraught.

Wife

Body and soul and all I am is yours.
If because we're poor, I lost patience,
it was not for my sake but for yours.
You have taken care of me in my hardships.
I refuse to let you be penniless.
I only wish that your soul
Were aware of my deepest thoughts.
When you express such opinions of me,
I feel depression in my soul and body.
I spit on silver and gold.
You live here in my soul and heart,
Are you going to leave me for a petty offense?
Leave me then! But … Oh, my soul
begs you to say you won't!
Do you remember when I was pretty as an idol
and you were my idolater?

Now your forgiveness would give me light.
I repent, I drop my opposition.
You're talking of separation — a bitter thing.
Do what you will, but don't do this.

She weeps in desperation.

✦

Chorus

From the rain of tears came a lightning flash
That shot a spark of fire in the lonely man's chest
She whose contempt shook your heart
What will you do when she weeps and falls apart?

If from the outside you dominate your wife
Inside you're dominated, seeking her love
The Prophet said that women prevail
With the intelligent and the wise
On the other hand it's the ignorant men
Who prevail over women

Those men cage inside them a violent beast
Love and compassion are traits of true humans
Greed and hatred are bestial traits.

Woman is a ray of God
Not the earthly lover she seems:
You might say she's not created — she's creator.

partoé haghast ân ma'shough neest
khâlégast ân gou'iya maklough neest.

✦

Bedouin

How did I become the enemy
of the woman who's the life of my soul?
Why am I kicking my soul in the head?
My wife — I'm the one who repents!
I have been an unbeliever. I must be a believer.
Now that I have stopped fighting you
do as you want. Draw the sword.
Whatever you ask me to do, I will obey:
I won't think of the consequences.
I will dissolve myself in you,
because I am the one who loves you.
Love makes a man blind and deaf.

A long pause.

Wife

I wonder: are you really my friend now?
Or are you trying to get me to spill my secrets
through some trick?

Bedouin

No, by the One who knows all hidden thoughts.

Wife *(becomes animated, takes his hands)*

A new sun has risen.
He is giving light to the whole world.
A new King, a Caliph of the merciful
has given the city of Baghdad an eternal spring.
If you gain access to this King,
you will become a king.

Bedouin

How am I going to be able to go meet the King?
How would I enter without some pretext?
I need some references. I need some means ...

Husamuddin (*forward, to the* Bedouin *and his* Wife)

For this gracious King to act,
the best means is to lack any means.
Having "means" involves pretense and self-promotion.
The heart of the matter is being empty of means:
to be nothing.

Bedouin (*to* Husamuddin *and the audience*)

How can I do business without means?
Unless I make a show of the fact that I have no means?

To his Wife.

Can you come up with some means to prove my lack of means?
So this wonderful King will take pity?

Wife

We have rain-water in the jug.
This is your property and your capital and your means.
Take this jug of water and go. Make it a gift
and go into the presence of the King of kings.

Bedouin

Who'd have thought we'd have such a gift as this?
This is truly a worthy gift for such a King.
Stop up the mouth of the jug.

Take care, for this is a gift that will bring us merit.
There is no water like this in all the world — none so pure.

Wife

You will carry it from the desert to Baghdad.
Oh God, let our pearl arrive at the sea!

✦

Chorus/Song (*English spoken & Persian sung*)

What is the jug? Our confined body
Holding the briny water of our senses.
A jug with five spouts.

cheest ân kouzé tané mahsouré mâ
andarou âbé havâssé shouré mâ
kouzé'i bâ panj louléy panj hess
pâk dâr in âb râ az har najess

Husamuddin & Seeker

The wife did not know that in Baghdad
there is a great river of water sweet as sugar
flowing like a sea through the city
full of boats and fishing nets.
You who live in this briny spring, how would you know
the Shatt and the Tigris and the Euphrates?
You who've not escaped from this fleeting caravansary
how would you know the meaning of words like
"self-extinction" and "intoxication" and "expansion"?
And those who do know them — it is by rote.

✦

The Story of an Exchange Between the Linguist and the Helmsman

Husamuddin picks up the book and holds it like a wheel at a ship's helm. He is now the Helmsman. Cloths like sails ripple in the wind. A daf, or frame drum, rolls with the sound of a storm. The Linguist with his book, is talking to the Helmsman at the wheel.

Linguist

How much farther.

Helmsman

With this storm, who can say?

Linguist

Shall we talk to pass the time?

Helmsman

S' all right with me.

Linguist

Have you ever studied linguistics?

Helmsman

What do you mean?

LINGUIST

It's my interest. I am a linguist.

HELMSMAN (*looking worriedly at the waves and skies*)

No.

LINGUIST

Well, then. You have squandered half your life.

Silence. The HELMSMAN *becomes sullen.*

LINGUIST

Have you nothing to say?

The wind is rising to a howl.

VOICES

Look out! Rough currents to starboard! Too late! We're caught! Haul down the life boat! Boat's gone overboard! Jump! We're going to hit the rocks! Jump! Jump!

LINGUIST

What's all that? What are they saying? Can't you hold this boat straight?

HELMSMAN (*to Linguist*)

Tell me, have you ever learned how to swim?

LINGUIST

No.

Helmsman

Mr Linguist, you have squandered your whole life.

✦

Husamuddin

If in this world you are the greatest scholar of your time
Take a look at how that world and that time pass away!
We have stitched in the story of the Linguist
To teach you the language of self-extinction.

To the Seeker.

Read.

Seeker

To be borne aloft and not to sink, you must learn to die.

Husamuddin

Let us see what became of the poor Bedouin.

✦

The Bedouin and His Wife: Part 3 — The Water Carrier

The Bedouin *arrives in the palace.*

Voice *(announcing his entrance)*

Come O Seeker! Bounty is in need of beggars. Bounty is needy like a Beggar!

Court Officials meet the Bedouin *graciously, and garland him with flowers.*

Official

O chief of the Arabs, where do you come from?
How are you, after such travels and exhaustion?

Bedouin

I'm a chief, indeed, if you'll do me just a favor.

On his knees, overwhelmed.

O ye in whose faces are the marks of eminence!
O ye whose splendor is more pleasing than the gold of Ja'far!
O ye, one sight of whom is seeing all the sights!
O ye at the sight of whom cold coins rain down!
O ye, all of whom have become seeing at the light of God!
Who cast the elixir of your looks on the copper
of untransformed individuals!

I am a stranger. I've come from the desert.
I've come in hope of gaining the good grace of the Sultan.
The scent of his grace seduced all the desert!
Even the grains of sands inhaled and gained souls!

Bring this gift to the Sultan.
Redeem me, the King's supplicant, from indigence.
It's sweet water and a new green jug—
fresh rainwater, collected in the ditch.

> The OFFICIALS *smile, look at one another, but receive the jug as if it were a precious object.*

✦

OFFICIAL

The Bedouin doesn't know about the Tigris.

2ND OFFICIAL

If he'd known about the Tigris,
he wouldn't have carried the jug so many miles.

OFFICIAL

No, if he'd known about the Tigris
he'd have smashed that jug on a rock!

> *The* SULTAN *appears. The* BEDOUIN *looks up and is unable to speak.*

SULTAN

I perceive what you want. I know what you have done.
Bring him back the jug, filled with gold.
Bestow a robe of honor on the man.

He calls the 1st Official to him.

Sultan

Put a jug of gold into his hands.
When he starts his trip back home, take him to the Tigris.
Say he has come here overland on the desert —
and it will be faster to return by this route.

✦

Young Woman *(with music)*

That jug of water points to different types of knowledge,
and the Caliph is the Tigris River of gnosis.
We are all bearing jugs of water to the Tigris.
If we do not know ourselves for the asses we are,
we really are asses!

✦

The Bedouin is at the banks of the Tigris with the Officials, standing before the boat that will take him home. He is speechless. He suddenly prostrates himself before the river.

Official One

This is your boat. Come, you will travel most of the way home this way.

Bedouin

Water.

OFFICIAL

Yes. The Tigris.

BEDOUIN

All fresh water?

OFFICIAL

Yes. Fresh water. Water for millions,
for boats and fishermen — for every use.

BEDOUIN

Wonders. This King's kindness is astonishing!
The greatest wonder is that he took our water!
How did a sea of benevolence like this man accept,
without blinking, such a dumb gift as my jug?

◆

THE WIFE *(with music)*

Each thing in the Universe is a jug
Brimming with wisdom and wonder
Each a drop of the Tigris of divine beauty
Which once was a hidden treasure:
Because of its fullness it burst forth
And made the earth more shining than the heavens

BEDOUIN

Had the Bedouin seen just a branch of this river
He'd have smashed the jug—smashed the jug
Those who see it are always beside themselves
Hurling stones at the jug of their self-existence

The jar is shattered, but no water is spilled
Nothing is lost: from this shattering
Hundreds of things are pulled together
Each atom of the jar is dancing in ecstasy
In this state neither jug nor water is manifest.

✦

Chorus

If you are attached to forms,
That is the worshiping of idols.
Let go of the forms and look at what is real.
If you are going on pilgrimage,
seek a pilgrim companion,
whether he be Indian or Turk or Arab.
Don't look at his form or his color.
Look at his purpose and intention.
If he is black and you are white,
you are still in accord:
you have the same spiritual complexion.

✦

Young Woman

This story has been told all twisted and wrapped around things. One can make neither head nor tail of it!

Husamuddin

Like people making love!
It has no head, since it's existed before eternity.
It has no foot, like the Eternal has no end.

The Elephant in the Dark House

A great wailing of flutes, pipes and drums.

The BAZAAR fills up with activity again. The stalls open. Stories are told. Much hawking and buying. An INDIAN DANCER enters.

The DANCER begins a dance in the Bharat Natyam style. She relates all events in mudra.

BAZAAR BARKER *(in Turkish and English)*
Ladies and gentlemen! Please come over to this corner.
We have a sight for you from the far reaches of Hindustan!

Some Hindus have brought an elephant for show!

Please step behind the curtain! Everybody in! That's right.
We shall now turn off the lamps. Let's go everyone.

All the merchants go in too.

The Elephant will now enter, but not until we turn out the light.
As elephants are not well known here, we ask you to describe it.

The lights go out.

The elephant please.

The sound of great plodding feet resonate in the room. The people gasp.

As seeing it with the eye is impossible,
please feel in the dark with the palm of you hands.

Do not fear, the animal will do you no harm.
Descriptions please! What is an elephant!

Voice 1

This animal is very much like — a water hose!

Voice 2

An elephant is … like a very flappy fan!

Voice 3

What I find here — I try to put both my arms around it — is that the elephant — is shaped like a pillar!

Voice 4

I am standing on a ladder and reach out my arm —
and it seems to me that it is actually not an animal —
but a very high throne.

Bazaar Barker *(with growing madness)*

If each one of you held a candle, you wouldn't be talking about such different animals! You see!
The eye of sense perception is only like the palm of the hand!
The palm doesn't have the power to grasp the whole elephant!
Day and night there are foam flecks on the surface of the sea!
You see the foam, but where is the sea?
Where is the sea! Marvelous! Ho! Look out!
We are dashing against each other, like boats in the night.
Our vision is murky, but we sail in sparkling water!

Voices

Well — turn on the lamps! Let us see!

Bazaar Barker (with growing madness)

You have gone to sleep in the boat of the body!
You have seen water — but have you seen the Water of the water?
Where were Moses and Jesus when the Source of Truth.
Poured water on the sown field of existent things?

Even my speech is imperfect and maimed.
It is only fragments of speech — whole speech is somewhere else!

Voices

The lights! — Turn on the lights! — The Elephant! Let us see!

The lights come on. The Elephant is gone.

Barker

If someone showed or told you the whole thing,
you would fall on your face!

The Crowd grows angry.

Crowd/Chorus

Madman —
We've been cheated! —
Report him to the authorities! —
Call the Police! —
Which authorities! —
Religious authorities!

Man

We describe an elephant! He tries to tell us about God!
We've all been taught who God is! How dare you utter these outrages!

Husamuddin has emerged from the crowd. The Young Woman accompanies him, wearing her veil.

Crowd/Chorus

Husamuddin! Chelebi! —
What would the Master say to this! —
A man who sets himself up as an authority! —
A false teacher! —
Give us the Master's words on this false religion!

Husamuddin *(Gestures for them to sit down)*
There is a story of Moses and a Shepard.

To the Seeker.

Go on. You have learned it.

He signals the Indian Dancer and the musicians to perform. The People sit in a large circle to watch.

How Moses Took Offense at a Shepherd's Prayer

As the Seeker *moves into her narrative of the Shepherd's tale, inside the circle around the book, the* Indian Dancer *from the previous scene performs classic mudra of caring for the Baby Krishna. She parallels the narrative and dialogue that follows. She eventually dances the story around the outer perimeter of the circle.*

Seeker

Moses saw a shepherd on his path, who was saying,

Seeker/Shepherd

"Oh God, who chooses whom you please
Where are You — I want to become Your servant,
and sew Your socks, fix Your small shoes and comb Your locks!
I want to wash Your clothes and pick out Your lice
and bring You milk, and worship you, my beauty!
I want to kiss Your small hand and rub Your delicate foot,
and when bedtime comes I want to sweep Your little room!"
You, for whom I'd sacrifice all my goats!
You in remembrance of whom I cry ay! ah!"
Moses said:

Husammudin/Moses

"Shepherd, to whom is this addressed?"

Seeker/Shepherd

"To that One who created us all!
The One who made the earth.
The One who made the sky."

Husamuddin/Moses

"Listen! You are depraved. In fact
you have not made yourself a true believer.
You've turned yourself into an infidel!
What babble is this? What is this raving blasphemy!
Stuff your mouth with cotton!
The stench of your blasphemy has made the earth stink.
Your blasphemy has turned the silk of religion into rags.
Shoes and socks may fit you fine,
but how are they useful for the sun!
If you don't shut-up, a fire will come and burn up the people!
To whom are you saying this? Your nieces or nephew?
Do you think the body and its needs
are attributes of the highest Glory?
The words: "He does not beget, nor was He begotten."
That's the proper description.
He exists before "begetter and begotten."
Birth is an attribute of everything that has a body.
Whatever is born is on this side of the river!"

Seeker/Shepherd

"O Moses!"

Chorus (*dissonant, sustained*)

"O Moses …"

Seeker/Shepherd

"You have sealed my mouth and burned my soul
with repentance!"
The shepherd tore his clothes and cried out with grief,
turned his face to the desert and hurried away.

> Now the INDIAN DANCER portrays the actions of Moses, as the
> WOMAN tells the tale.

A revelation came to Moses from God.
"You have parted my servant from me.
Did you come as a prophet to unite, or to sever?
If you can help it, do not go the way of separation.
Of all things, I loathe division most!
I have bestowed on everyone a special way of being:
I have given to everyone a unique form of expression.
For him his words are worthy of praise,
for you they would be worthy of blame.
For him honey, for you poison.
I am beyond purity and impurity.
For Hindus the forms of Hind have value.
For Sindhis the forms of Sind have value.
I'm not concerned with tongue and speech.
It's the inward spirit and the inward state.
I gaze into the heart
Because heart is the essence,
speech is arbitrary
the essence is what's real.
How many more phrases
and concepts and metaphors?
I want burning, burning:
become close with that burning!
Light up a fire of love in your soul.

Burn thought and expression all away!
O Moses, the ones who know the Law are one sort:
those whose souls and spirits burn are another sort!

When Moses heard these reproaches,
he ran into the desert looking for the shepherd.
He pushed onward, following the footprints of the bewildered man.
Desert dust flew up around his feet.
The footsteps of a distraught man are, in fact,
different from other footsteps.
One step is like the rook in chess, moving from top to bottom.
With the next step he goes cross-ways like the bishop.
First lifting his crest like a wave,
then going on his belly like a fish,
His feet writing his state in the dust,
like a geomancer who finds omens by lines in the sand.
At last Moses saw him and caught up with him.
The giver of good news said:

Husamuddin/Moses

"Permission is granted.
Do not seek any rules or method of worship.
Say whatever serves your anxious heart.
Your blasphemy is true religion,
and your religion is the light of the spirit.
You are saved and through you a whole world
is in process of being saved."

Seeker/Shepherd

"O Moses, I have passed beyond that.
I am now bathed in my heart's blood.
I have passed beyond the lotus tree, beyond all distance.
I have taken a hundred thousand years' journey on the other side.

You plied the lash, my horse shied,
made a leap and passed beyond the sky.
I want my Divine Nature to be close with my human nature —
Blessings be upon you!
My state right now is beyond this description."

◆

HUSAMUDDIN *(to the Assembly in the market. The Ney plays.)*
You examine an image in a mirror.
It is your image, not the image of the mirror.
The breath which the flute-player blows into the flute —
does it belong to the flute? No, it's the flute-players'.
One day, when the veils are removed,
how you will say over and over —

CHORUS

"This is not what they were thinking."

END OF ACT I.

Photo: Page Carr

Act II

How Some Sufis Sold a Traveler's Donkey to Pay for a Night of Music

Seeker
If our senses don't tell us the truth, how can we ever know it?

Husamuddin
Recite "The Night of Music."

Young Woman
A Sufi, after a long journey, arrived at a Sufi Khanegha.
He took his mount and led it to the stable
And there he made sure it was given food and water,
taking precautions that nothing would go awry —
but in matters of destiny, what use is precaution?

✦

Visitor *(to a Servant)*

Please make sure he has hay and water this evening
and first thing in the morning.

Servant

God willing.

Visitor

What do you mean by that. Please ensure
that he is brushed and prepared for riding in the morning.

Servant

God willing.

✦

Husamuddin

These Sufis were poor and destitute: The very existence
of poverty is infidelity that leaves the soul in shambles.
O you rich and well-fed man, beware of laughing
at the unrighteous acts of the suffering poor.

> The Dervishes, joined by Husamuddin and the Young Woman/Seeker welcome the Visitor into their circle.

Visitor

Thank you for your hospitality. In God's name.

Dervishes

In God's name you are welcome.

The Visitor removes his shoes and cloak. He goes to a corner and stands in a tableau of "freshening up." The Dervishes sit in their circle.

Dervish One *(whispers to another)*

In case of dire need, a carcass is lawful food.

Dervish Two

There is many a vicious act that necessity made a virtuous one.

Dervish One

Which means we should sell the ass.

Dervish Two

The one he put up in the stable.

Dervish One

Then we shall purchase a good meal. A worthy meal.

Frieze.

✦

Seeker

They quickly sold the little ass. They fetched meats of great delicacy and lit many candles.

✦

Dervish One

Tonight we'll have music and dancing and delicacies
and amazing feasting!

Dervish Two

How much more of this wandering with the begging bowl?

Dervish Three

How much more of this patience!

Dervish Four

And these three-day fasts!

Dervish One

We are also beings and souls who need to live.

Dervish two

Tonight luck is with us.

Dervish Three

We have to entertain our guest.

Dervish

Friend! Here you are!

> *The Dervishes descend on the visitor with great friendliness, serving him tea, playing music. They crowd around him and get him to dance.*

Visitor

If I don't celebrate a bit tonight, when?
The smell of the kitchen is exquisite.

The musicians play, the SERVANT *has served them all and everyone sets to eating with their hands. Eventually the music stops. Out of the silence, a* DERVISH *sings:*

DERVISH

The ass is gone
The ass is gone
The ass is gone
The ass is gone

The others join in and clap. The daf and drums start in. The group is sitting, and begins an extended interlude of music, in which many get up and dance with a "beating of feet, the tumult of soul, caused by longing and ecstasy." They wave their hands above their heads, "they beat the ground with their feet; they sweep the dais with their foreheads."

DERVISHES *(impassioned)*

The ass is gone
The ass is gone
The ass is gone
The ass is gone … etc.

The VISITOR, *at first startled, eventually joins in, with full fervor.*

DERVISHES *(joining in, clapping)*

The ass is gone
The ass is gone
The ass is gone
Oh son! Oh son! etc.

This goes on a long time till the jumping and revolving and ecstasy reaches anarchy.

The VISITOR is swept up, rises and dances, urging on the rest of the group. The SERVANT comes in, and tries to speak in the VISITOR's ear over the din, but is gestured away. She/He tries several times, and finally leaves, or takes part in the revelry.

ALL

The ass is gone
The ass is gone …
Etc.

It continues until it reaches a frantic pace, till the final ecstatic falls to the floor asleep. Silence. The light goes down.

◆

Morning light. Slowly people struggle to get up. Rub their eyes, etc. People stagger out.

THE VISITOR

Farewell. And thank you, my friends.

DERVISH ONE

Farewell.

DERVISH TWO

A pleasant journey to you. God willing.

He retrieves his bags, and looks out in the direction in which the servant took the ass to tie him up the previous day. He does not see his ass.

Visitor

The servant has taken the ass out for water,
it drank so little last night.

> *Then he sees the servant still asleep on the floor.*

Visitor

Where is the ass?

Servant

Look at your beard.

Visitor

Don't get smart. I entrusted the ass to your care.

Servant

God willing.

Visitor

Enough of that. I put you in charge of the ass.
Give me some answers, not your smart talk.
I demand from you what I gave you, or we'll go to see the Cadi.

Servant

I was overpowered. Those Sufis rushed me,
and I was in fear for my life.
Do you throw a liver among cats and expect to see
a trace left of it the next day?

Visitor

If they attacked you with violence, to take the ass,
they might've been aiming at my life.

And seeing this you did not come to me and say:
"They are taking away your ass, you poor man!"
I could have bought back the ass!
Or I could have let them divide my money and return my ass!
There were a hundred ways to fix things —
but now all those people have vanished into the blue!
How could you not come to me and say,
"An awful crime has happened?" To the Cadi!

Servant

By God! I came several times to inform you of all this
But you kept repeating over and over
"The ass is gone! The ass is gone, oh son!"—
with more gusto than the rest of them.
I thought: "He himself is aware. He is satisfied with destiny.
He is a man of unfathomable wisdom."

Visitor (*disconsolate*)

They all were singing it with such joy,
that it filled me with joy too, when I sang.
Blind imitation has brought me to ruin.
Two hundred curses on imitation!

The Person Who Imagined Seeing the New Moon

Gentle music. Ney. Santur.

Seeker

Once in Omar's time, when the month of fasting came
some people ran to the top of a hill
to have the luck of being the first to spot the new moon.

Moon Gazer

One of them said: "Look, Omar! There's the new moon!"

Omar

Omar, not seeing the moon in the sky said:
"This moon has risen out of your imagination.
Otherwise, since I am more practiced at
watching the heavens than you
why can't I see the pure crescent?
Wet your hand and rub it on your eyebrow
and look again for the new moon."
When the man wetted his eyebrow
he could not see the moon.

Moon Gazer

"My Lord. There is no moon.
It has disappeared."

Omar

Yes, the hair of your eyebrow
was curved downward like a bow
and shot you with an arrow of false opinion."
One crooked hair prevented true seeing.

The Frozen Snake

Chorus

A Snake Catcher!

Percussion.

The Snake Catcher *has entered the playing area, and begins his travels up hill and down dale on his journey as he speaks.*

Snake Catcher

A snake catcher went to the mountains
to catch a snake with incantations.
Whether one is slow or quick,
he that's a seeker will be a finder.

Chorus/All

Always throw yourself with both feet into seeking
the searching itself is the best guide on the path.

Snake Catcher

The snake-catcher sought the snake
in order to find friendship.

Chorus

A man seeks a snake for a friend
to care for something that has no care for him.

Snake Catcher

The snake-catcher was searching in the mountains
For a big snake in winter snows.
There he caught sight of a long dead serpent
The sight of which filled him with dread.

Chorus

Snake-catchers catch snakes to astonish the public
Ah, The Foolish Public!

Snake Catcher

The snake-catcher packed up the serpent
and went to Baghdad to stir up excitement.

He rolls him in a rug.

Chorus

For a trifling fee he'd carry about this serpent
like a pillar of a house, and said:

Snake Catcher

"Here you have a dead serpent, which could only
be brought here by overcoming odds and agony."

Chorus

He thought it was dead, but it was living, and
he hadn't inspected it very well.
It was frozen by frosts and snow. It was living
though it gave the appearance of being dead.

Husamuddin

The World appears frozen — inanimate — it is called *jamâd*.
But, sir, for "frozen" we say — *jâmid*.
When the sun of the resurrection rises
you will see the body of the World in motion.

Chorus

Finally the showman arrived in Baghdad
and set up for his spectacle at the crossroads.
He presented his show on the banks of the Tigris
and word-of-mouth made a stir in the town.

Bazaar Barker

"A snake-catcher has brought a serpent here,
he has discovered a strange and marvelous beast."
Gullible hordes who were now his prey,
as he was prey to stupidity, gathered to see the serpent.

Chorus

The bigger the crowd, the better the begging
and donations of cash.

Bazaar Barker

Streams of empty-headed babblers gathered round
up on tiptoe, packed like sardines.
Men and women pressed together
classes mingled in the crowd
like nobles and common folk on Resurrection Day.

Snake Catcher

As he started to lift the cloth cover over the serpent,
the crowd strained their necks

and saw that the serpent, frozen by severe cold
lay beneath a hundred wool blankets and covers.
He had bound it with thick rope:
he had taken every precaution.

Chorus

The sun of Iraq beat down on the snake.
The blood in its limbs unfrosted
It was dead. Now it revived: the serpent uncoiled.
When the dead serpent moved the public's amazement
grew by leaps and bounds.

Serpent

They ran off screaming, while the ropes binding the serpent
went crack and then crack, one after the other.
It burst its bonds and glided out on the ground
a hideous dragon roaring like a lion.

> *The chorus runs back and forth across the space,
> in waves of fear. The* Serpent *stands over the book at
> center, kicking and thrashing like a ninja.*

Serpent

A multitude were killed in the melee:
a hundred piles of the slain were stacked.

Snake Catcher

The snake-catcher was paralyzed with fear, crying:
"What have I brought here from the wastelands?"

Serpent

The blind sheep had awakened the wolf
and unwittingly went to its angel of death.
In one gulp the serpent sucked down that dolt.
It wound itself round a pillar and crunched
his bones in its belly.

Chorus

The serpent is your compulsive self, the ego: you think it's dead?
It shuts down only when denied the means to thrive.
If it is given those means by a power like Pharaoh
then it will act like Pharaoh and pull down
hundreds like Moses and Aaron.

Serpent

Keep the serpent in the snow of separation from its desires.

Chorus

Take care not to take it to the Sun of Iraq … !

The Man Who Prayed for an Income without Labor in the Time of King David

The market-place materializes again. Noise, bargaining and people bark about their goods.

A man ("Do-Nothing") comes out before a market stall, and begins calling out on his knees. After his first exclamation, the crowd goes silent.

Do-Nothing

O God! Give me riches without having to trouble for it!
Since you made me a do-nothing,
a coward, a milksop, a dull-wit, a sluggard
it can't be expected that an ass like me with a sore backside
can carry a horse's load!
Since you have made me a lazy man
let me earn my daily bread by my vocation: doing nothing!
I am inert — sleeping in the shade of existence.
Surely for such people you have prescribed another livelihood.
Everything that walks on its feet seeks a livelihood:
show pity on someone with no foot at all.
The baby has no feet to walk on, and its mother comes
and pours forth milk.
I have deep need of daily income which just appears!
Without wear and tear on me.

Solemnly, in prostration.

Because my only work is seeking.

Some people pass his stall.

Chorus Member 1

Fantastic. You hear what this idiot is saying?
Is he stupefied from too much hashish!

Chorus Member 2

Everyone has been given an occupation
and a capacity for finding one.

Chorus Member 3

The King and divine messenger of our time is David.
No one has deeper knowledge.
His miracles are countless. The tides of his bounty
come to us like wave after wave.

Chorus Member 4

Despite all his majesty, God saw fit to give him a livelihood
linked to his seeking and his mission.

Chorus Member 5

Without weaving coats of mail, without exerting effort
he has no livelihood — despite all his victories.
Then a lunatic like this comes out saying
"I will climb up to the sky without a ladder!"

Chorus Member 6

Go and get it! Your "income" — your daily bread — has arrived.
The messenger has come with the good news!

Chorus Member 2

Give us a share — village bigshot!

◆

Seeker

He never ceased his annoying prayers,
and made his wishes known out loud despite abuse and ridicule.
And so he became a celebrity in the town,
as the man who sought cheese from an empty lunchbucket.
This beggar was a living parable on foolishness.
He went on many long nights,
with a hundred forms of supplication.

> *The Chorus/Crowd in the market laughs.*
> *Do-Nothing keeps up his praying, unbothered.*
> *Crowd/Chorus breaks up, leaving the man alone. A silence.*
> *Chorus (Bellows like a cow.)*

Do-Nothing

A cow! In my house!

> *The Do-Nothing jumps up and quickly grabs a great knife, and with sudden forceful determination, runs out in the direction of the cow, wielding a sword. A great bellowing is heard.*

> *Chorus bellows and shrieks.*

> *The Do-Nothing returns without the knife.*

Do-Nothing

I must get to the butcher. He will skin her for me.
Every part can be sold.

Seeker (*emerging from the* Chorus)

People are fools. I do not know what to think.
These are the vain and selfish desires the book warns of.

Husamuddin

There's danger in judging from outward acts.
Our Master said:
"Come seek, for seeking is the foundation of fortune.
Success consists in having the whole heart fixed upon an object."

Seeker

The heart and desire seem so dangerous. They can make you a fool and a do-nothing.

✦

The Owner *of the cow encounters the* Do-Nothing *on his way.*

Owner

Hey you! That was my cow you've gone and killed. Criminal!
Come on, let's have it out! Why did you kill my cow?
Idiot and thief! Out with it!

Do-Nothing

I was begging God to provide me with my daily bread,
and I was completely focused upon this prayer.
The cow was my income. I killed her.
Behold. The answer to your question.

The OWNER picks him up by the collar and strikes his face back and forth with his hand several times.

The OWNER then picks the DO-NOTHING up and makes him walk.

OWNER

Come on you blind idiot. Come on criminal!
We'll see what King David says to your stupid story.
What kind of prayer is that, you say?
You're mocking my beard and your own at the same time, rascal!

DO-NOTHING

I've gone through much pain and work
to get the answer to my prayer.
Go break your head on the rocks, foul-mouthed man!

OWNER

Hey, gather round, righteous people!

The CHORUS/CROWD gathers.

Listen to the drivel and ravings of this imbecile!
He killed my cow!
Can anyone explain how prayer
should make my property belong to him?
If that were so, with a single prayer like his,
the whole world would be seizing
each others' possessions by force.
Supplication and prayer are the means for blind men
to earn their livelihood. Yet they get no gifts.
Just crusts of bread!

Chorus/Crowd

This man is speaking the truth. —
This prayer-monger's committed an injustice. —
How can you pray to acquire property! —
Where is that in the law! —
Give back the cow or go to prison!

Do-Nothing (*on the ground*)

No one but You knows my inner experience.
You put the prayer in my heart!
You raised a hundred hopes in my heart!
That impostor has called me blind because of this crime!
But when have I been praying the prayers of the blind?
When have I begged from anyone but the Source?
This blindness of mine is the blindness of love.
As they say, "Love makes a man deaf and blind."
Just as You once showed a dream to honest Joseph,
and it became a support to him,
You've blessed me with a dream too.
That endless prayer of mine was no sham acting.

Owner

Turn your face to me! Tell the truth!
Why are you turning your face to heaven, old man!
You are a fraud, you are spreading lies,
you are babbling about love and your nearness to God.
Since, you are spiritually dead inside,
you have some face to turn your face to the heavens!

The Chorus/Crowd *becomes angry, grabbing stones and tools.*

The Do-Nothing *throws himself prostrate on the ground.*

Do-Nothing

O God, do not put me, your servant, to shame.
Even if I am wicked, do not divulge my secret.
My supplications are worth nothing in the eyes of these people.
In Your eyes they shine like a lamp.

He is dragged brutally to the palace of David. *The* Chorus/
Crowd *is shouting.*

The doors open, and David *steps forward, raising his hand to quiet
the* Crowd.

David

All right. What's this all about? What is it?

Owner

Oh prophet, give me justice! My cow strayed into his house.
He killed my cow. Ask him to explain what happened.
And ask him why he killed my cow!

David

Speak up, you grand fellow! How did you destroy
the property of this good citizen?
Take care. Don't beat around the bush.
Tell me how you plead, so that this case may be settled
and put to rest.

Do-Nothing

Oh, David. For seven years I spent day and night
in invocation and prayer.
"Oh God," I said, "I want a means of livelihood,
that will be lawful, and cost me no effort."
Men and women both know about my sorrow and how I cried aloud.

The children can tell you.
Ask whomever you like for information about this.
Ask them openly or secretly what this beggar
in his tattered cloak was saying.
After all my invocations — suddenly I saw a cow in my house.
I killed her as alms in thanks that the One
who knows things unseen could hear my prayer.

David

Strike those words from the record.
And you, declare a legal plea in this dispute.
Do you think it right for me to establish a bad precedent in Jerusalem
by not demanding your plea?
Who gave you this cow? Did you buy or inherit her?
How can you dare sell the crop, are you the farmer?
Understand, my good man: that acquiring property is like farming.
If you do not sow the land, the produce does not belong to you.
For you reap what you sow. That is yours.
Otherwise, your action is unjust, and we find against you.
Go, pay this good man's money, and no more lies.
Go try to borrow, pay him back, and do wrong no more.

Do-Nothing

Oh, King, you are saying the same thing to me
that the oppressors say.

He prostrates himself. The Chorus/Crowd *yells and threatens.*

Do-Nothing

Oh, You who know my inner flame,
cast it into the heart of David!

He begins to weep and lament loudly. David *is disturbed.*

David *(to the Owner)*

Listen — you, the one demanding justice for his cow.
Give me a little time today,
and we'll go no further into the matter under dispute,
So that I can go into seclusion and contemplation —
to reach the Knower of mysteries.

> *Tableau.* David, *isolated in light,*
> *Music, ney or santur. Or the Persian below is sung simultaneously.*

David

For then the window of my soul is opened,
and in the purity of the Unseen World,
the divine Book comes to me without intermediary.
The Book and the rain of the spirit and the Light
fall through the window of my house from the true Source.
The house that is without a window is Hell.
Don't you know that the light of the sun
is the reflection of the Sun beyond the veil?
I am plunged in Light like the sun.
I cannot distinguish myself from the Light.
My going to prayer and solitude
is for the purpose of teaching the people the Way.

Singer *(simultaneously)*

rowzané jânam goshâdast az safâ
meeréssad beevâssété nâméy khodâ
nâmé vo bârâno nour az rowzanam
meefétad dar khâné-am az ma'danam
douzakhast ân khâne kân beerowzanast
asslé din éy bandéh rowzan kardanast
man cho khorsheedam darouné nour ghargh

meenadâm kard kheesh az nour fargh
raftanam souyé namâzo ân khalâ
bahré ta'leemast rah mar khalgh râ
kazh naham tâ râst gardad in jahân
harb khod'eh in bovad éy pahlavân

David

I put things crooked so that this world
might become straight.

✦

Husamuddin

We're not permitted give more words to David here,
or he might reveal the whole matter.
He might raise a dry path through the sea of mystery.

✦

The litigants and the Chorus/Crowd gathers before David's door. The plaintiff, the Owner, is yelling at the Do-Nothing and threatens to lay hands on him.

David

Be silent! Go, give up your claim,
and acquit this devout man of responsibility for your cow.
The fact is, God has thrown a veil over you!
Go, and observe silence, and be thankful
that who you are is concealed.

Owner

Oh, my God! What kind of judgment is this?
What justice? Are you changing the whole Law
for my case only?
The fame of your justice has given fragrance
to earth and heaven!
Even blind dogs don't suffer wrongs like this!
Rocks and mountains explode at this injustice!
Listen all of you! The time of injustice has come!
The time of injustice has come!

The Crowd/Chorus (*Muttering. A man yells.*)

Injustice!

David

You greedy, grasping man.
Give all of your wealth to him this instant.
Otherwise your situation will become grave.
Your crimes can come to light through him.

Owner (*tears his shirt and throws dust over his head*)

Every word adds insult to injury!

He runs about the crowd, tearing at himself, yelling.

David

Please bring him here …
Since you were not fated to be saved …
You're banished. Get out of here!
Your children and your wife will now be this man's servants.
Leave them. Say no more!

The Owner begins dashing his own body with a pair of stones.

The Chorus/Crowd becomes restless, angry. The women begin wailing, and the men shouting at the obvious injustice. They begin beating on the ground and the walls with wooden stocks and tools, in rising revolt.

They freeze in tableau.

✦

The Seeker cries out. She moves about the characters in the frieze.

Seeker

How should someone who is subject,
like straw in the winds of passions,
know the oppressor from the oppressed?

Husamuddin

He who cuts off the head of his deluded self —
only he learns to distinguish oppressor from oppressed.
Otherwise the true oppressor, the commanding self within you,
moves toward frenzy — that is the adversary of the oppressed.
A wild dog always attacks the poor,
and if it can, inflicts wounds upon the poor.
Understand that lions feel shame, but not sick dogs.

Seeker

The mob, which slays the oppressed
and worships the oppressor —
their dog-soul leaps forth …

✦

The Crowd, *now a* Mob, *rush at* David, *wielding their stocks, crying out. Even so, they are divided amongst themselves.*

Chorus/Crowd

O chosen prophet! —
You who had compassion on us! —
This is unworthy of you! —
This is clear injustice! —
You have torn down an innocent man for nothing! —
Injustice!

David

Friends. The time has come
that the plaintiff's hidden secret should be revealed.
We go — all of us — so that we may
become acquainted with that secret.
Out on the plain there, is a great tree,
its boughs dense and curved.
From its roots the smell of blood is coming to me.
Murder was committed beneath that tree:
a man with a dark destiny once killed his master.

Drums. Ritual walking. Percussion. Finally, they arrive at the "tree."

David

Tie his hands behind his back,
and I will bring his crimes to light, in the name of justice.
You dog! You have killed this man's grandfather.
You were a servant, but by this route
you've become esteemed by your wealth.
You killed your employer and took his property:
the Knower has made clear what happened to him.
Your wife was his handmaid. She has been party

to the injustice against him too.
Now you'll serve him all your life.
Your gains and goods are his property.
You demanded the law: you will have your law.
You used gross violence to kill your employer,
while he was begging for mercy on this very spot.
In your haste you buried the knife in the ground.
Now — both your master's head and the knife
are in the ground here! Dig up the earth, there!

> *Three of the* MEN *dig furiously in the ground. A knife is produced. Cries of dismay.*

On the knife you'll find the name of this dog here,
who dealt his master both lies and pain.

> *A* WOMAN *gives out a cry. A head has been pulled up from the ground. Then a wailing goes up from the people, who are beside themselves.*

CROWD/CHORUS

We've been blind from birth! —
With three pebbles and a sling
he drove off an army of a hundred thousand! —
The stones spoke to him to take them against Goliath! —
And we abuse him! —
It was you who abused him! —
The mountains play music with David! —
They chant his Psalms with him! —
Through his breath a thousand eyes are opened! —
He opens people's eyes to the Unseen!

David

Come on, you, obsessed with calling for "Justice! Justice!"
Receive the justice due to you!

He holds THE OWNER's *knife in the air.*

In this cycle of suffering the ignorant and the greedy
tear their masks off by their own actions.
Saying: "Behold me! My ego has horns!
Now you see the inner cow in full view!
The beast of hell!"

✦

Chorus

A hundred thousand eyes were opened, David, through your
    breath,
and were opened to meditation on the Unseen.
That miracle is stronger than all these others,
for it's the one that lasts.
You bestow the life that lasts on the dead souls.
This is in fact the heart of all miracles.

Husamuddin

Slay your ego and make the world come alive.

Chorus

Your ego has killed it's master.
You must make it serve you.

Husamuddin

Listen to me! Your ego is like the man suing for his cow.

Chorus

It has made itself commander.
The slayer of the cow is your clear-thinking self:
do not be offended with the slayer of the ego-cow.
The intellect is a prisoner,
but still craves an income for nothing.
On what does this income-for-nothing depend?
Upon its slaying the "cow"
which is the origin of all evil.

> *The* Chorus *moves backwards into shadows in the market. They begin closing the stalls, until the chamber is no longer "the market" but a circular void. They have removed themselves to the circle of the beginning, motionless.*

✦

Seeker

Master? What do we do?
They all retreat from the truth!
They don't know they're carriers of the water.
The water we are all taking to the sea.
Why is it such a secret? People can't tell
what is precious from what is counterfeit.
David calls for ritual sacrifice.
What good does sacrifice do?

Husamuddin

I make sacrifice. I sacrifice my self.
Each of my limbs is a way to raise free spirits from the dead.
Slay this cow — the commanding self —
if you want to bring to life the spirits of insight.

Seeker

Is that our Master speaking or you?

Husamuddin

Both.

Rites of Return: Wedding the Beloved

Seeker

For love I've got to lose myself.
For love I have got to die before I die.
I am afraid. I feel like I'm a burning house!
And now our Master is nowhere …

Husamuddin

I heard his voice cry out out — through you.
When you, too, are nowhere, you will wake up.

Seeker

Awake and nowhere.

Husamuddin

When you wake there is nothing present.
Only Presence.
Like the breath present in the ney.
That's what's contained in the syllable "hu".

The Ney begins to play.

Husamuddin

You are about to become a bride.
Marry non-existence and be reborn in Reality.

"The sound in the ney is not wind but fire."

Wedding gown and death shroud, the same garment.
Practice dying in love.
Practice dying in love.

   Music begins.

Husamuddin

The Vakil of Bukhara fled his King in fear of his life
for having offended him. But his love made him return,
even at the cost of his death. When he returned,
the Vakil found his beloved King returning his love,
reaching — reaching — reaching out for him
until he felt himself die. Then, finally, he could live.
Practice dying in love.

> *He lets go of her hand and leaves her standing shrouded in white in the empty hall. She stands alone radiating white in the dark, in the same shaft of light that hits the illuminated book. The dark grows ever denser, and the white of her garments glow ever whiter as she shines in increasingly black space.*

> *The Chorus reemerge one by one and drape the Young Woman in white and gold garments. Each recites one stanza as they drape her, and back away to their place in the circle.*

I was once a mineral and then I died
And became a form that learned how to grow

I was once a plant and then I died
As growing flora and became an animal

I was once an animal and then I died
And became human: Why fear? I've never lost by dying.

I will die as a human one day I shall die
So I shall lift my head and soar as an angel.

Once more as an angel again I shall die
And what I'll then be is beyond imagining.

Then I'll die once more into non-existence.
Why fear? I've never lost by dying.

> *The Music takes flight. Then stops. Silence.*

✦

> *Whispering, in waves, with an individual voice rising above the others then sinking back into the soft sea of voices.*

Chorus

This is the book of the Mathnavi, which is the roots of the roots of the roots of the Religion in respect of its unveiling of mysteries of attainment to Truth … The likes of the light thereof is as a niche in which is a candle shining with radiance brighter than the dawn. It is the heart's paradise, having fountains and boughs … for the travelers on the Path …

End

Afterword: Why Put Rumi on Stage?

Open Theatre/DC undertook its first tour of *Rumi's* MATHNAVI from February to April of 2005, throughout the Washington-Baltimore-Philadelphia area. Each performance followed by "Peace Talks." The following discussion by Joe Martin appeared in *Pathways*, Spring 2005.

Q To start with the obvious question: why put a medieval Persian poet like Jelaluddin Rumi on stage in America?

A Rumi may have created his masterwork the *Mathnavi* in the thirteenth century, but in this part of the world, compared to Europe of the time, it was more like the Renaissance. It was a golden age of Islam, and was certainly a major pinnacle for Sufism in the Islamic world, when Sufi thought influenced in a major or lesser way the majority of Muslims. The Sufis were at the heart of this golden age beginning in the 9th to 10th centuries. That was the time when Ibn Sina (Avcenna) established the field we call medicine in both the east and the west. He was also a peripatetic philosopher (a branch of

Sufism). So the question is like "Why do Shakespeare? He is five hundred years old." But he is the pinnacle of the Western Renaissance.

Q Shakespeare was the great poet of the Western Renaissance. But he wrote for the stage. Rumi wrote for reading, study and introspection, did he not?

A Rumi's *Mathnavi* was created in singing lines, called, in fact, "mathnavis." These were twenty-two syllable lines with middle and end rhyme. In a sense, like rhymed couplets in the West. From his own life time (he died in 1270 CE) they have been performed by one or several singers, with musical accompaniment, in chai houses, in Sufi locales, shrines of Sufi saints where such performances are common, in formal concerts. When it comes to the *Mathnavi* many of the stories are dramatically dynamic parables. Conventional theatre was not widespread in Rumi's area of the world, apart from passion plays about Hussein's life, or the Karagoz shadow puppets in Turkey.

Q But why theatre? Isn't Islam against "representation?"

A At its origins, in the Prophet's time, the tradition was in fact taken from the Old Testament and the Jewish prophets. At that time, 99% of all art portrayed divine and religious subjects. The great Islamic calligraphers, miniaturists, poets and composers, especially in the Persian and Turkish areas became free once art branched into other subjects, as were Jewish artists. Current fundamentalist arguments against art notwithstanding.

Q But isn't the comparison with Shakespeare straining to mix apples with oranges?

A This is not what I want to talk about here. But let's just say that Rumi is by analogy the closest thing to a Shakespeare of the Middle East and Central Asia, at least in that sense that we call Shakespeare "the Bard." Furthermore, despite Rumi's spiritual objectives — he was the greatest of spiritual guides and is still called Mowlana (our teacher) in the Middle East — his *Mathnavi* examines society from top to bottom as Shakespeare did. He is concerned with illumination and the connection with the divine. However, he returns again and again to the market place. It's the place of intrigues, of selling and buying, of cheating, power plays, beggars, poets and performers, prince's fools and holy men.

Q But Rumi's, or Mowlana's poetry, you have just said, was written for spiritual purposes.

A Yes.

Q That's certainly not very Shakespearean.

A True. Unless you also see Shakespeare as the Bard of love — as in his sonnets which can be compared to Rumi's ghazals written on love, or his devotion to his spiritual comrade Shams-i Tabriz. It's also in his romances and comedies. But very much like Shakespeare's take on the quest for power and the destructive force of egotism, Rumi goes into the darkness of human compulsions and power lust. For his two spiritual aims are to heighten awareness and also to quell the ambitious ego. He acknowledged that darkness and the power of the ego are part of the whole picture.

Q Shakespeare sometimes adored the ego. Look at Falstaff.

A Because the ego is both trickster and fool, and is therefore highly theatrical. Rumi too finds the ego and its folly entertaining and compelling. Remember. Lear's ego made him a fool, as is underscored in that play forty times. Othello too. But really, our point here is not to turn Rumi into Shakespeare.

Q Then that brings us back to the initial question. If the tales and parables of the *Mathnavi* were not written for theatre, why undertake this sort of theatre project?

A Because Rumi, it turns out, is a voice for our times.

Q Simply because he has sold more books of poems in America in one decade than any other poet?

A No. Because he represents the quintessence of all spiritual wisdom traditions, from any religion you might name.

Q But there are other great writers who are representatives of these traditions: Bashō, Milarepa, even the Dalai Lama.

A For that matter we have the parables of Jesus and Shakyamuni Buddha — but in several ways they do not address the most threatening issues before us today in the same way.

Q They all teach us about the interconnectedness of existence. Doesn't that more or less cover all the issues?

A Yes. In the language of the Sufis in Islam the interdependence of beings is called Wahdat al-Wujud (Unity-of-Being). It is everywhere in Rumi's work, not the precise term, but the concept.

Q That makes him equally valuable to us right now in times of fragmentation. But more valuable?

A Yes and no. In our time those leaders and thinkers drawn to polarization and dualism, to make themselves "powers to be reckoned with" have adopted the notion of an inevitable "clash of civilizations."

Q What do you mean, "adopted?" Some would say we need only to look at the nightly news to see that the clash of civilizations is a fact.

A It's a fact based upon the promotion of a very big myth, which serves the interests of extreme people on both sides. When Rumi died, the streets of Konya (his home in Turkey) were filled with crowds of Greek and Anatolian Christians and the Jews of Konya, along with his Muslim followers, lamenting his loss. Like the Dalai Lama today, Rumi's orientation within Islam did not prevent him from suggesting that people were often better off in their own spiritual traditions. In whatever spiritual tradition one adhered to, the importance is sincerity rather than self-righteousness. (Which is the dominant "symptom" from which the people promoting the clash of civilizations suffer.) In the *Mathnavi* he writes: The ways of Sindh are appropriate for Sindhis / The ways of Hind are appropriate for Hindus." He is referring to Muslim and Hindu areas of the subcontinent. He also has many tales and parables about the Jewish prophets. But as a Muslim he was profoundly affected by the figures of Jesus and Mary. For Christ is a figure fully saturated with the Spirit, and is a stand-in for all of us and our ultimate potential:

> Every night I escape this four branched cross
> And spring away from this stop-over in prison
> Into the wide pasture of the spirit.
> — VI.222

In Mary's conceiving Jesus, Rumi also sees potential for all human beings, and that the soul is essentially feminine in nature:

> The Universal Soul came into contact with the
>   partial soul
> and the separate soul received a pearl from it
> and held it to her breast.
> Through that touch on its breast the separate soul
> became
> pregnant like Mary,
> with a Messiah that would charm the heart,
> not the Messiah who travels on land and water
> but the Messiah who is beyond limitation or space.
> So when the soul has become impregnated by
> the Soul of the soul
> by such a soul the world itself
> becomes pregnant.

Q Surely you can't claim that such thinking describes the Islam of today.

A When Professor Abdul Aziz Said, who helped broker the

Oslo Peace Accords, was asked by the *Washington Post* what Rumi would have said in encountering Osama Bin Laden, he responded: "You are a stranger to Islam." From the time of the great jurist and Islamic philosopher Al Ghazzali, one of the greatest, he deemed Sufism to be key to Islam, the Sufis have been able to claim they are the inner core of Islam. Without this inner kernel, the outer shell, the rituals and code of conduct, becomes twisted and empty. And this has happened to some today.

Q   What does Rumi have to say to those outside of Islam. And what does he offer to those who cannot adhere to any institutionalized religion whatsoever.

A   Well, here is his famous welcome, which goes something like this: "Come whoever you are / Be you religious / be you fire worshiper or idol worshiper / Come / Even if you have broken vows a hundred times / Come." Then there is the famous refrain from a great poem. "Don't go back to sleep."

Q   Meaning?

A   Rumi's *Mathnavi* arose as a sort of massive six-volume reflection on the inner meaning of the Koran. But, as said, it draws from the Gospels, the Torah, the Hindu Panja Tantra, which is a book of fables, and many other sources, including Greek philosophy. But for humanity in general his concern is consciousness, which in his use of language is inseparable from God. That is, whichever of the ninety-nine names of the divine you apply: Allah, Truth, Essence, Majesty, Mind. Allow me to quote him one more time:

> Since consciousness is the inmost nature and essence of the soul,
> The more aware one is the more spiritual she is.
> Awareness is the effect of the spirit:
> Anyone who has this in abundance is a part of God.
> — VI.149-50

Q And a text charged with these perceptions can be read, sung, or performed on a stage for people?

A Well, let me go straight to the horse's mouth again: "Have you not heard that the present life is only a play?"

Q And the "clash of civilizations?"

A People are looking for too many villains in the play — outside of the power-seeking ego.

About the Author

Playwright, novelist and theatre director, Joe Martin's works comprise an international, curious, formal exploration into the border regions between the spiritual cosmos and the political world. He has lived or sojourned in Norway, Sweden, Canada, Mexico, India, Turkey, Tunisia, Nepal and France and received several grants and awards as a writer and director — including a Fulbright Senior Fellowship in Theatre, and grants from the Rockefeller Foundation, the American Scandinavian Foundation, the DC Commission on the Arts and Humanities. In 2002, he was selected as a Fulbright Senior Specialist in Theatre.

Martin's original works and translations have been published and produced around the US, Canada, England and Mexico. His recent books include *Foreigners, Conspiracies: Six Plays, Strindberg, Seven Plays, Keeper of the Protocols: The Works of Jens Bjorneboe*, and *Parabola* (Asylum Arts). Author and adapter of some thirty plays, including *The Dust Conspiracy, The Receiver, Anatole's Lover, The Match Girl's Snow Queen*, and *Rumi's Mathnavi*, for fifteen years he has directed Washington's laboratory theatre, Open Theatre/DC. Also active as a translator of drama from Swedish, Norwegian and Spanish, he has translated many works of August Strindberg, as well as Jens Bjorneboe, and Juan Tovar.

A director and dramaturg of over fifty stage productions in the US, Canada and Europe, his choices have included both originals and classic works such as *Jose Rivera's Marisol* (Bucharest, 2002) and Strindberg's *A Dream Play* (Washington, DC, 2003). He is a Lecturer in the Theatre Program at Johns Hopkins University, and in Creative Writing at George Washington University.

www.ingramcontent.com/pod-product-compliance
Lightning Source LLC
Chambersburg PA
CBHW070122080526
44586CB00013B/1353